CAROLINE LUCAS

The Biography and Inspiring Journey of a Woman Who Transformed UK Politics

Kisha Grande

All rights reserved. No part of this publication may be reproduced, distributed,or transmitted in any form or by any means, including photocopying, recording, or other electronic or mechanical methods, without the prior written permission of the publisher, except in the case of brief quotations embodied in critical reviews and certain other noncommercial uses permitted by copyright law.

Copyright © Kisha Grande, 2024.

Table of Content

Introduction..5
Chapter 1..11
  The Trailblazer......................................11
- Early life and influences...............11
- The Journey Into Politics............ 13
- Election as the UK's first Green Member of Parliament in 2008.. 17

Chapter 2..19
  Standing Firm..19
- Challenging Westminster Norms.. 19
- Refusing to Conform to Party Lines..22
- Representing the Concerns of Constituents................................. 24

Chapter 3..27
  Principles in Action.............................. 27
- Advocacy for the NHS, Schools, Railways, and More.......................27
- Prioritizing Local Jobs and Communities................................ 29

- The Fight for Affordable and Secure Housing in Brighton........32

Chapter 4..**35**
   Climate Crusader.. 35
- Radical Action and Environmental Advocacy............35
- Promoting Renewable Energy and Initiatives................... 38
- Promoting Renewable Energy and Green initiatives.................. 40
- From Coastal Preservation to Wildlife Conservation.................43

Chapter 5..**46**
   Political Views & Other Roles................... 46
Chapter 6..**50**
   The Personal Side.. 50
Conclusion.. **51**

Introduction

In the annals of political history, few figures stand as boldly against the grain as **Caroline Lucas**. Born into the idyllic backdrop of Malvern, Worcestershire, on December 9, 1960, Lucas emerged from humble beginnings with a sincere conviction that the world could be better. Raised in a household steeped in the values of social justice and environmental stewardship, her formative years were imbued with a sense of responsibility to challenge the status quo and advocate for change.

Armed with an insatiable curiosity and an unyielding spirit, Lucas embarked on a journey of intellectual exploration at the University of Exeter. Here, she honed her analytical prowess and cultivated a deep-seated passion for literature and language, laying the groundwork for a career that would defy convention and redefine the landscape of British politics.

But it was not merely academic pursuit that fueled Lucas's fire—it was a burning desire to confront injustice head-on and champion the causes that resonated with her core principles. Stepping into the political arena, she found her voice amidst the cacophony of Westminster, where conformity often overshadowed conviction. Yet, Lucas refused to be silenced, determined to carve out a space for authentic representation and unwavering advocacy.

With each stride she took, Lucas shattered stereotypes and shattered barriers, blazing a trail for a new brand of politics—one rooted in integrity, compassion, and unwavering commitment to the common good. From the hallowed halls of Parliament to the bustling streets of her beloved Brighton, she has remained a steadfast beacon of hope, inspiring generations to dare to dream of a world where justice, equality, and sustainability reign supreme.

As we embark on this journey through the life and legacy of Caroline Lucas, let us be reminded that true change begins with a single voice, a single act, and a single vision. And in the story of Caroline Lucas, we find not only the embodiment of that truth but a rallying cry for all who dare to believe that a better world is not just possible—it is inevitable.

In the following pages, we will go deep into the extraordinary life and legacy of Caroline Lucas, a woman who defied convention to become a towering figure in British politics. Throughout this biography, several themes will emerge, offering insight into the values, motivations, and impact of one of the most influential voices of our time.

1. Defiance of Convention: From her earliest days, Caroline Lucas was anything but ordinary. Born into a family that prized social justice and environmental stewardship, she embarked on a path less traveled, challenging the norms of the political establishment and refusing to be constrained by the confines of tradition.

2. Integrity and Authenticity: At the heart of Caroline Lucas's journey lies a steadfast commitment to integrity and authenticity. In a world where political expediency often trumps principle, she has remained true to her convictions, earning admiration and respect from allies and adversaries alike.

3. Advocacy for Change: Throughout her career, Lucas has been a tireless advocate for change, championing causes ranging from environmental sustainability to social justice. With passion and determination, she has fought to give voice to the voiceless and address our time's pressing issues.

4. Environmental Leadership: Perhaps most notably, Caroline Lucas has emerged as a leading voice in the fight against climate change and environmental degradation. With a deep understanding of the urgency of the crisis, she has spearheaded efforts to promote sustainability and protect our planet for future generations.

5. Empowerment of Communities: In her role as a Member of Parliament for Brighton Pavilion, Lucas has worked tirelessly to empower communities and to amplify the voices of her constituents. Through grassroots organizing and community engagement, she has sought to build a more inclusive and participatory democracy.

6. Legacy and Inspiration: As we reflect on the life and work of Caroline Lucas, we are reminded of the enduring power of principled leadership and the profound impact that one individual can have on the world. Her legacy serves as an inspiration to all who dare to dream of a better future and to strive for positive change.

As we embark on this journey, let us be guided by the principles of courage, compassion, and resilience that have defined Caroline Lucas's remarkable life. Through her story, we find hope, inspiration, and a roadmap for building a more just and sustainable world for generations to come.

Chapter 1

The Trailblazer

Early life and influences

Caroline Lucas was born in Malvern, Worcestershire, to parents Peter and Valerie Lucas. Her upbringing was in a middle-class household where her father ran a small central heating business and sold solar panels, while her mother focused on raising their three children.

She attended Malvern Girls' College, a boarding school in Great Malvern, before earning a first-class Bachelor of Arts degree in English Literature from the University of Exeter in 1983. During her university years, Lucas actively participated in the Campaign for Nuclear Disarmament (CND), joining protests at Greenham Common Women's Peace Camp and Molesworth Peace Camp. She was particularly involved in the Snowball Campaign against US military bases in the UK, which sometimes led to her engaging in civil disobedience.

Lucas then pursued further studies at the University of Kansas, where she earned a Diploma in Journalism on a scholarship between 1983 and 1984. Returning to the University of Exeter, she completed a PhD in English in 1990 with a thesis titled "*Writing for Women: a study of woman as reader in Elizabethan romance*."

During her doctoral studies, Lucas worked as a press officer for Oxfam starting in 1989. She continued her involvement with Oxfam in various capacities while also becoming increasingly active in the Green Party. Eventually, she left her role at Oxfam in 1999 to focus more on her political career.

The Journey Into Politics

Inspired by **_Jonathon Porritt's_** seminal work "_Seeing Green_," Caroline Lucas made a pivotal decision to join the Green Party in 1986. Living in Clapham at the time, she felt a compelling urge to commit herself wholeheartedly to the party's ideals. Shortly thereafter, Lucas assumed key roles within the party, serving as its National Press Officer from 1987 to 1989, and later as Co-Chair from 1989 to 1990.

Reflecting on her early days in the party, Lucas emphasized the importance of substance over style in a 2009 interview with Decca Aitkenhead of The Guardian. She highlighted the evolving perception that attire should not detract from the substance of one's message—a shift she observed during her tenure.

With the Green Party's division into separate entities for the constituent parts of the United Kingdom in 1990, Lucas aligned herself with the

Green Party of England and Wales. Her dedication to the cause was further evident as she assumed the role of General Election Speaker in 1991, preparing for the subsequent year's general election, and later serving as a Regional Council Member from 1997 onwards.

Lucas's electoral breakthrough came with her successful bid for a council seat on Oxfordshire County Council, marking a significant milestone in her burgeoning political career. Holding this position from 1993 to 1997, she demonstrated her commitment to effecting change at the local level, laying the groundwork for her future endeavors as a formidable force within the Green Party.

Caroline Lucas made her initial foray into elected office as a Member of the European Parliament for the South East England Region in 1999, a significant milestone coinciding with the introduction of proportional representation in European elections. The Green Party's strong showing, capturing 7.4% of the vote with

110,571 votes, marked a turning point in Lucas's political trajectory.

However, her principled stance on nuclear disarmament led to a notable episode in November 2001 when she was convicted of breaching the peace during a CND sit-down protest at the Faslane nuclear base in Scotland. Defending herself in court, Lucas argued fervently for the right to peaceful protest enshrined in the Human Rights Act, underscoring her unwavering commitment to anti-nuclear activism.

Despite the legal challenges she faced, Lucas continued to garner electoral success, securing re-election in 2004 and 2009 with increasing vote shares. Her tenure in the European Parliament saw her take on key roles in committees addressing trade, industry, energy, environmental policy, and climate change, further solidifying her reputation as a formidable advocate for progressive causes.

Beyond her legislative responsibilities, Lucas demonstrated leadership in advancing global initiatives such as the International Simultaneous Policy (SIMPOL), aimed at breaking the deadlock in addressing pressing global issues. Additionally, she actively engaged in intergroup collaborations focusing on animal welfare, peace issues, consumer affairs, and relations with ACP countries and the Palestinian Legislative Council.

In 2008, Lucas's commitment to environmental sustainability and economic justice led her to join the Green New Deal Group, advocating for transformative policies to address the interconnected challenges of recession, climate change, and energy insecurity. Her leadership within the Green Party, including stints as Female Principal Speaker, underscored her role as a driving force for progressive change both within the party and on the international stage.

Election as the UK's first Green Member of Parliament in 2008

Caroline Lucas made history on September 5, 2008, when she was elected as the Green Party's inaugural leader, securing an overwhelming mandate with 92% of the vote. Before her leadership, the party had functioned under a collective leadership model, but Lucas's election marked a strategic shift towards a more recognizable and relatable figurehead.

Explaining the rationale behind the change, Lucas emphasized the importance of personal connection in communicating political ideals to the public. She recognized that while abstract ideas may have their place, it is often individuals who embody those ideas that resonate most with people.

Lucas's leadership tenure saw the Green Party make significant strides, culminating in her historic election as the party's first Member of Parliament for Brighton Pavilion in the 2010 general election. However, her leadership was not without controversy, as evidenced by her vocal support for campaigners involved in the Smash EDO campaign, which resulted in damage to an arms factory. Lucas defended their actions as a legitimate response to the atrocities in Gaza, underscoring her unwavering commitment to peace and justice.

In subsequent years, Lucas continued to make her mark on the political landscape, notably voting against military intervention in Libya in 2011. Despite her successes, she announced her decision to step down as leader in May 2012, citing a desire to create opportunities for new voices within the party and to elevate the profiles of aspiring leaders. Reflecting on her tenure, Lucas expressed pride in the progress the Green Party had made under her leadership, heralding a new era of influence and impact for the party.

Chapter 2

Standing Firm

Challenging Westminster Norms

In the hallowed halls of Westminster, where tradition and conformity often reign supreme, Caroline Lucas stands as a beacon of defiance against the status quo. As the Member of Parliament for Brighton Pavilion, she has carved out a reputation as an unconventional lawmaker, unafraid to challenge the entrenched norms of political culture.

Lucas's approach to politics is refreshingly unorthodox, rooted in a steadfast commitment to authenticity and integrity. Unlike many of her colleagues, she refuses to be bound by the constraints of party politics or beholden to vested interests. Instead, she remains fiercely independent, guided solely by her principles and the best interests of her constituents.

This unwavering commitment to principle has earned Lucas a reputation as a maverick within Westminster's corridors of power. Whether it's speaking truth to power on issues of environmental sustainability, social justice, or peace activism, she consistently refuses to compromise her values for the sake of political expediency.

But Lucas's defiance extends beyond mere rhetoric—it is reflected in her actions. From her early days as an activist with the Campaign for Nuclear Disarmament (CND) to her vocal opposition to military intervention in Libya, she has never shied away from taking a stand, no matter how unpopular or controversial.

Yet, it is not just in opposition where Lucas's strength lies; it is also in her ability to champion positive change. As a vocal advocate for environmental sustainability, she has spearheaded efforts to combat climate change and promote renewable energy initiatives. Her leadership on issues such as divestment from fossil fuels and protection of natural habitats has garnered widespread acclaim and inspired countless others to join the fight for a greener, more sustainable future.

In a political landscape often characterized by cynicism and compromise, Caroline Lucas stands as a rare beacon of hope. Her unwavering commitment to principle, coupled with her fearless advocacy for positive change, serves as a reminder that true leadership is not measured by the size of one's majority, but by the strength of one's convictions. As we delve deeper into her journey in the following pages, we will uncover the many ways in which Lucas's steadfastness has reshaped the landscape of British politics and inspired a new generation of changemakers.

Refusing to Conform to Party Lines

Caroline Lucas's tenure as an MP has been marked by her unwavering commitment to independence and integrity, principles that have guided her actions and decisions in Westminster. Unlike many politicians who toe the party line without question, Lucas has consistently demonstrated a willingness to stand apart, unafraid to challenge orthodoxy and advocate for what she believes to be right.

At the heart of Lucas's approach is a deep-seated belief in the importance of remaining true to one's principles, even in the face of pressure to compromise. Throughout her career, she has refused to be swayed by political expediency or the allure of power, choosing instead to prioritize the interests of her constituents and the causes she holds dear.

This steadfast independence has often put Lucas at odds with her own party, particularly on issues where she believes they have fallen short of their principles. Whether it's opposing military interventions, advocating for stricter environmental regulations, or championing social justice causes, she has never hesitated to speak out, even when it meant standing alone.

But Lucas's commitment to independence goes beyond mere rhetoric—it is reflected in her actions. As the first Green MP in the UK, she has consistently defied expectations and broken new ground, proving that it is possible to be both principled and effective in politics.

In a system where loyalty to party often takes precedence over individual conscience, Lucas's refusal to conform has earned her both admiration and criticism. Yet, she remains steadfast in her conviction that true leadership requires the courage to stand up for what is right, even when it is unpopular or inconvenient.

Representing the Concerns of Constituents

In the bustling coastal city of Brighton, Caroline Lucas has become more than just a Member of Parliament—she is a tireless advocate, a trusted voice, and a champion for the concerns of her constituents. From the moment she was elected as the MP for Brighton Pavilion, Lucas made it her mission to be a steadfast ally and a fierce defender of the people she represents.

At the core of Lucas's approach to governance is a deep-seated commitment to listening and engaging with the diverse voices of her community. Whether it's attending town hall meetings, hosting public forums, or simply walking the streets of Brighton, she has made it a priority to be accessible and responsive to the needs and aspirations of those she serves.

But Lucas's advocacy for Brighton goes beyond mere rhetoric—it is backed by tangible action and results. From securing funding for vital local projects to championing causes that directly impact the lives of residents, she has proven time and again that she is willing to roll up her sleeves and fight for what matters most to her constituents.

Whether it's advocating for improved public transportation, fighting for affordable housing solutions, or pushing for greater investment in education and healthcare, Lucas has consistently put the needs of Brighton at the forefront of her agenda. Her unwavering dedication to the people she represents has earned her a reputation as a fierce and effective advocate, someone who is willing to go to bat for her constituents, no matter the odds.

In a political landscape often characterized by cynicism and detachment, Lucas's hands-on approach to representation stands as a beacon of hope. By centering her work on the concerns and priorities of the people of Brighton, she has redefined what it means to be a true public servant, someone who is not just in office to hold power, but to make a meaningful difference in the lives of those she serves.

Chapter 3

Principles in Action

Advocacy for the NHS, Schools, Railways, and More

In the turbulent landscape of contemporary politics, Caroline Lucas stands as a steadfast defender of the public services that form the bedrock of our society. From the National Health Service (NHS) to our schools and railways, she has been a tireless advocate for ensuring that these essential services remain accessible, affordable, and of the highest quality for all.

At the heart of Lucas's advocacy for public services lies a deep-seated belief in the principle of equity and social justice. She understands that access to healthcare, education, and transportation is not just a matter of convenience, but a fundamental human right that must be protected and preserved for future generations.

In her role as an MP, Lucas has consistently fought to safeguard the NHS from privatization and austerity-driven cuts. She has been a vocal critic of government policies that undermine the integrity of our healthcare system, pushing for increased funding, improved access to services, and greater support for frontline workers.

Similarly, Lucas has been a staunch defender of our education system, advocating for adequate funding, smaller class sizes, and greater investment in teacher training and support. She recognizes that education is the key to unlocking opportunity and empowering individuals to reach their full potential, and has worked tirelessly to ensure that every child has access to a high-quality education, regardless of their background or circumstances.

But Lucas's advocacy for public services extends beyond healthcare and education to encompass our transportation infrastructure as well. She has been a vocal proponent of renationalizing the railways, arguing that public ownership is essential for ensuring affordability, reliability, and sustainability in our transportation networks.

In every battle she has fought and every cause she has championed, Caroline Lucas has remained true to her principles and unwavering in her commitment to protecting and preserving our public services.

Prioritizing Local Jobs and Communities

In her relentless pursuit of a fairer and more sustainable society, Caroline Lucas has placed a strong emphasis on building a resilient economy that puts people and communities first. At the core of her approach is a recognition of the vital role that local businesses and jobs play in fostering economic stability and prosperity.

Lucas understands that vibrant local economies are the lifeblood of thriving communities. That's why she has been a tireless advocate for policies that prioritize the creation and protection of local jobs, particularly in sectors such as renewable energy, sustainable agriculture, and small-scale manufacturing.

One of Lucas's key initiatives has been to promote the development of renewable energy projects as a means of both combating climate change and stimulating economic growth. By investing in clean energy infrastructure and supporting local renewable energy cooperatives, she has sought to create sustainable jobs while reducing our dependence on fossil fuels.

Additionally, Lucas has been a vocal proponent of supporting small businesses and entrepreneurs, recognizing their importance as engines of innovation and economic vitality.

Through initiatives such as community-led regeneration projects and support for local procurement policies, she has worked to create an environment where small businesses can thrive and contribute to the prosperity of their communities.

But Lucas's vision for a resilient economy goes beyond just creating jobs—it's also about ensuring that those jobs provide fair wages, decent working conditions, and opportunities for advancement. She has been a staunch advocate for policies such as the living wage, worker cooperatives, and employee ownership schemes, which empower workers and promote economic equity.

By prioritizing local jobs and communities, Caroline Lucas has demonstrated her unwavering commitment to building an economy that works for everyone, not just the privileged few.

The Fight for Affordable and Secure Housing in Brighton

In the city of Brighton, where soaring property prices and a shortage of affordable housing have created a crisis for many residents, Caroline Lucas has emerged as a fierce advocate for ensuring that everyone has access to safe, affordable, and secure housing.

Lucas understands that housing is not just a basic human need—it's a fundamental human right. That's why she has made it a priority to address the housing affordability crisis head-on, advocating for policies that prioritize the needs of renters, low-income families, and marginalized communities.

One of Lucas's key initiatives has been to push for stronger rent controls and tenant protections to prevent exploitation and ensure that renters are not priced out of their homes. She has been a vocal supporter of measures such as rent stabilization, longer tenancy agreements, and restrictions on evictions, which are essential for providing stability and security to renters in an increasingly precarious housing market.

Additionally, Lucas has championed efforts to increase the supply of affordable housing in Brighton, working to secure funding for the construction of new affordable homes and the renovation of existing properties. She recognizes that addressing the housing crisis requires a multifaceted approach that includes both short-term interventions and long-term planning to ensure that everyone has a place to call home.

But Lucas's advocacy for affordable housing goes beyond just policy proposals—it's also about amplifying the voices of those most affected by the crisis. She has worked closely with housing activists, community organizations, and grassroots campaigners to elevate their concerns and push for meaningful change at both the local and national levels.

Through her tireless advocacy and unwavering commitment to housing justice, Caroline Lucas has become a beacon of hope for renters, homeowners, and those experiencing homelessness in Brighton.

Chapter 4

Climate Crusader

Radical Action and Environmental Advocacy

In an era defined by the existential threat of climate change, Caroline Lucas has emerged as a leading voice in the fight for environmental justice and sustainability. As a staunch advocate for radical action to combat the climate crisis, Lucas has dedicated her career to raising awareness, driving policy change, and mobilizing communities to take urgent and decisive action.

At the heart of Lucas's environmental advocacy is a deep-seated belief in the need for transformative change. She understands that incremental measures and half-hearted commitments are no longer sufficient to address the scale of the challenge we face. That's why she has been a vocal proponent of bold, ambitious policies that prioritize the rapid transition to a low-carbon economy and the protection of our natural world.

One of Lucas's key initiatives has been to push for legislation that sets ambitious targets for reducing greenhouse gas emissions and transitioning to renewable energy sources. She has been a tireless advocate for measures such as carbon pricing, renewable energy incentives, and investments in clean technology, which are essential for driving the systemic changes needed to mitigate the worst impacts of climate change.

But Lucas's climate crusade goes beyond just advocating for policy change—it's also about inspiring grassroots action and mobilizing communities to become part of the solution. Through initiatives such as community-led renewable energy projects, tree planting campaigns, and youth climate activism, she has worked to empower individuals and communities to take ownership of their role in the fight against climate change.

Additionally, Lucas has been a vocal critic of the fossil fuel industry and corporate interests that continue to prioritize profits over the planet. She has called for an end to subsidies for fossil fuel companies, divestment from fossil fuel investments, and greater accountability for corporations that contribute to environmental degradation.

By leading the charge against climate change with passion, determination, and unwavering commitment, Caroline Lucas has become a beacon of hope for environmentalists, activists, and concerned citizens around the world.

Promoting Renewable Energy and Green Initiatives

Caroline Lucas's commitment to combating climate change extends beyond advocacy—it's about driving tangible change through sustainable policy solutions. Recognizing the urgent need for a transition to renewable energy and green initiatives, Lucas has been at the forefront of promoting policies that prioritize sustainability and environmental stewardship.

Central to Lucas's approach is the promotion of renewable energy sources as a viable and necessary alternative to fossil fuels. She has championed policies that incentivize the development and adoption of renewable technologies such as solar, wind, and hydroelectric power. By advocating for subsidies, tax incentives, and investment in renewable energy infrastructure, Lucas aims to accelerate the shift away from fossil fuels and towards a cleaner, more sustainable energy future.

But promoting renewable energy is just one aspect of Lucas's broader vision for sustainability in policy. She has also been a vocal advocate for green initiatives across various sectors, from transportation to agriculture to waste management. By promoting policies that prioritize energy efficiency, sustainable transportation options, and eco-friendly agricultural practices, Lucas seeks to reduce carbon emissions and minimize the environmental impact of human activity.

Moreover, Lucas recognizes that achieving sustainability requires a holistic approach that considers the interconnectedness of social, economic, and environmental factors. That's why she advocates for policies that promote social justice, equity, and inclusivity alongside environmental protection. From supporting initiatives to address environmental racism and frontline community empowerment to advocating for a just transition for workers in fossil fuel industries, Lucas aims to build a more equitable and sustainable society for all.

Through her advocacy for sustainability in policy, Caroline Lucas is not only working to combat climate change but also to create a world that is healthier, more resilient, and more equitable for future generations.

Promoting Renewable Energy and Green initiatives

Caroline Lucas's dedication to sustainability in policy is rooted in the belief that transitioning to renewable energy and promoting green initiatives are essential steps towards mitigating the impacts of climate change and creating a more sustainable future.

One of Lucas's key strategies for promoting renewable energy is through advocating for policies that support the development and adoption of renewable technologies. This includes initiatives such as offering financial incentives for renewable energy projects, streamlining permitting processes for renewable energy installations, and investing in research and development to improve the efficiency and affordability of renewable energy technologies.

In addition to promoting renewable energy, Lucas is a strong proponent of green initiatives across various sectors of society. This encompasses policies aimed at reducing carbon emissions, conserving natural resources, and promoting sustainable practices in areas such as transportation, agriculture, and waste management. By advocating for measures such as increased public transit options, sustainable farming practices, and recycling programs, Lucas seeks to foster a culture of environmental stewardship and responsibility.

Moreover, Lucas recognizes the importance of integrating sustainability into all aspects of policymaking. This means considering the environmental impacts of legislation and decision-making processes across government departments and sectors. By promoting policies that prioritize sustainability, Lucas aims to create a regulatory framework that encourages businesses, organizations, and individuals to adopt more environmentally friendly practices and behaviors.

Ultimately, Lucas's advocacy for sustainability in policy is driven by a commitment to safeguarding the planet for future generations. By promoting renewable energy and green initiatives, she seeks to not only address the urgent challenges of climate change but also to build a more resilient and sustainable society that values the health and well-being of both people and the planet.

From Coastal Preservation to Wildlife Conservation

Caroline Lucas's environmental advocacy extends beyond national and global issues to the protection of Brighton's unique and diverse environment. As the MP for Brighton Pavilion, she has been a staunch defender of the city's natural landscapes, wildlife habitats, and coastal areas, working tirelessly to ensure their preservation for future generations.

At the forefront of Lucas's environmental efforts in Brighton is the preservation of its coastal areas. Recognizing the ecological significance and cultural importance of Brighton's coastline, she has been a vocal advocate for measures to protect it from erosion, pollution, and unsustainable development. Through initiatives such as beach clean-ups, coastal restoration projects, and advocacy for stricter regulations on coastal development, Lucas seeks to safeguard Brighton's beaches and shorelines for the enjoyment of residents and visitors alike.

In addition to coastal preservation, Lucas is committed to wildlife conservation in Brighton and beyond. She recognizes the importance of protecting and enhancing biodiversity in urban environments, which provide vital habitats for a wide range of plant and animal species. From advocating for the creation of wildlife corridors and green spaces to supporting initiatives to protect endangered species and their habitats, Lucas aims to ensure that Brighton remains a thriving ecosystem where wildlife can flourish.

Moreover, Lucas's environmental advocacy in Brighton encompasses efforts to address pressing environmental issues such as air and water quality, waste management, and climate resilience. By promoting policies that reduce pollution, improve waste management practices, and mitigate the impacts of climate change, she seeks to create a healthier and more sustainable environment for all residents of Brighton.

Through her unwavering commitment to protecting Brighton's environment, Caroline Lucas has demonstrated her dedication to preserving the natural beauty and ecological integrity of the city for future generations.

Chapter 5

Political Views & Other Roles

Caroline Lucas's multifaceted involvement in various organizations and causes reflects her unwavering commitment to advocating for social, environmental, and humanitarian issues.

As Vice-President of the Royal Society for the Prevention of Cruelty to Animals (RSPCA), Lucas demonstrates her dedication to animal welfare. Additionally, her role on the National Council of the Campaign for Nuclear Disarmament (CND) underscores her commitment to peace and disarmament efforts.

Lucas's engagement extends to parliamentary groups such as the All-Party Parliamentary Group on Peak Oil and Gas, where she serves as Vice Chair, highlighting her interest in sustainable energy and environmental policy.

Moreover, her membership in groups like the All-Party Parliamentary Group for Choice at the End of Life and the All-Party Parliamentary Group for Drug Policy Reform reflects her advocacy for compassionate and evidence-based approaches to sensitive social issues.

Beyond her parliamentary duties, Lucas contributes to numerous advisory boards and think tanks, including the International Forum on Globalisation and the Centre for a Social Europe, where she lends her expertise on trade justice, globalization, and environmental sustainability.

A prolific writer and advocate, Lucas's publications and speeches on trade justice, localization, and environmental concerns demonstrate her commitment to challenging neoliberal ideologies and promoting sustainable alternatives. Her book "Green Alternatives to Globalisation: A Manifesto," co-authored with Mike Woodin, advocates for local economies and greater environmental consciousness in opposition to the forces of globalization.

Lucas's support for causes such as the People's Assembly Against Austerity and her endorsement of Jeremy Corbyn's leadership campaign in the Labour Party underscore her commitment to social justice and progressive change.

Furthermore, Lucas's advocacy for a universal basic income and her active participation in campaigns such as the People's Vote demonstrate her commitment to empowering individuals and promoting democratic engagement.

Despite facing criticism and challenges, such as the investigation by the Parliamentary Commissioner for Standards, Lucas remains steadfast in her dedication to holding government accountable and advocating for transparency and integrity in public office. Her successful legal action against the Department of Health and Social Care over contracts awarded during the COVID-19 pandemic highlights her commitment to ensuring fairness and accountability in government decisions.

Lucas's activism extends to issues of gender equality and ending violence against women. Her participation in campaigns calling for greater awareness of male violence against women and girls reflects her commitment to addressing systemic issues of gender-based violence and discrimination.

Despite facing challenges and criticism, Lucas remains a steadfast advocate for social and environmental justice, consistently pushing for progressive policies and systemic change. Her diverse portfolio of engagements and unwavering dedication to advocating for a more just, equitable, and sustainable world inspire others to join her in the fight for positive change.

Chapter 6

The Personal Side

Caroline Lucas and Richard Savage exchanged vows in 1991, marking the beginning of their journey as a family. They take pride in raising two sons, one of whom has embarked on an academic path at the University of California, Santa Barbara, reflecting their shared enthusiasm for learning and knowledge dissemination.

In her personal life, Lucas embraces vegetarianism and has openly discussed her transition toward a vegan lifestyle. During a candid conversation with ITV News Political Correspondent Paul Brand in September 2019, she affirmed her dedication to ethical and sustainable living practices by expressing her commitment to this dietary shift.

Conclusion

As Caroline Lucas bids farewell to her parliamentary career, her legacy as a trailblazing politician and advocate for change shines brightly. From her historic election as Britain's first Green MP to her relentless advocacy for social and environmental justice, Lucas has left an indelible mark on UK politics.

Her courage to challenge the status quo, whether through grassroots activism or bold parliamentary interventions, has inspired countless individuals to join the fight for a better world. As she embarks on the next chapter of her journey, we can be sure that Caroline Lucas will continue to lead by example, championing causes close to her heart and inspiring generations to come.

Though her time in Parliament may be drawing to a close, the spirit of Caroline Lucas's unwavering dedication and tireless pursuit of a more equitable and sustainable future will undoubtedly endure as a beacon of hope for us all.

Printed in Great Britain
by Amazon